I Can Do It, I l ,

Hope Blecher-Sass
Highland Park, New Jersey

Illustrations by
E. Silas Smith

Dominie Press, Inc.

All authors' royalties from the sale of the *Teacher's Choice Series* will be used to support various early literacy projects throughout the United States.

Publisher: Raymond Yuen
Editor: Bob Rowland
Designer: Jon Reily
Series Editor: Stanley L. Swartz
Illustrator: E. Silas Smith

Published by:

Dominie Press, Inc.

1949 Kellogg Avenue
Carlsbad, California 92008 USA

ISBN 0-7685-0116-4

Printed in Singapore
14 15 16 17 18 VoZF 15 14 13

"Let me help you put on
your shoes and socks," said Dad.
"No, thanks. I can do it,
I really can," said Armando.

“Let me help you put on
your coat and boots,” said Mom.
“No, thanks. I can do it,
I really can,” said Armando.

“Let me help you cut
that shape,” said the teacher.
“No, thanks. I can do it,
I really can,” said Armando.

"Let me help you write
your name," said the teacher.
"No, thanks. I can do it,
I really can," said Armando.

"Let me help you count
to ten," said the teacher.
"No, thanks. I can do it,
I really can," said Armando.

"Let me help you with your backpack,"
said the principal.
"No, thanks. I can do it,
I really can," said Armando.

“Let me help you turn on the water,” said Mom.
“No, thanks. I can do it, I really can,” said Armando.

“Let me help you with your pajamas,” said Dad.
“No, thanks. I can do it,
I really can,” said Armando.

“Can I help you with anything?” asked Mom.
“You can read me a story,” said Armando.
“I can do it, I really can,” said Mom.

About the Author

Hope Blecher-Sass is an ESL (English as a Second Language) teacher for the Edison Township Public School District, in Edison, New Jersey. She attended Bergenfield Public Schools, and earned her bachelor's degree from Cook College/Rutgers University and her master of arts from Rider College and Kean College. Hope also has three certifications as: Teacher of the Handicapped, Teacher of ESL, and Teacher of Elementary Education. During her thirteen-year teaching career, she has taught students in kindergarten through twelfth grade. Hope has participated in many volunteer projects, including Science Alliance, NTTI, and the New Jersey Museum of Agriculture. She also has developed programs and worked with her peers to incorporate students, parents, and businesses in the promotion of literacy. Hope lives in Highland Park, New Jersey with her husband, Raymond, and her daughter, Loren. She enjoys reading mysteries and telling stories to Loren. Hope says she is an example of a person who was read to as a child and who still reads every night.